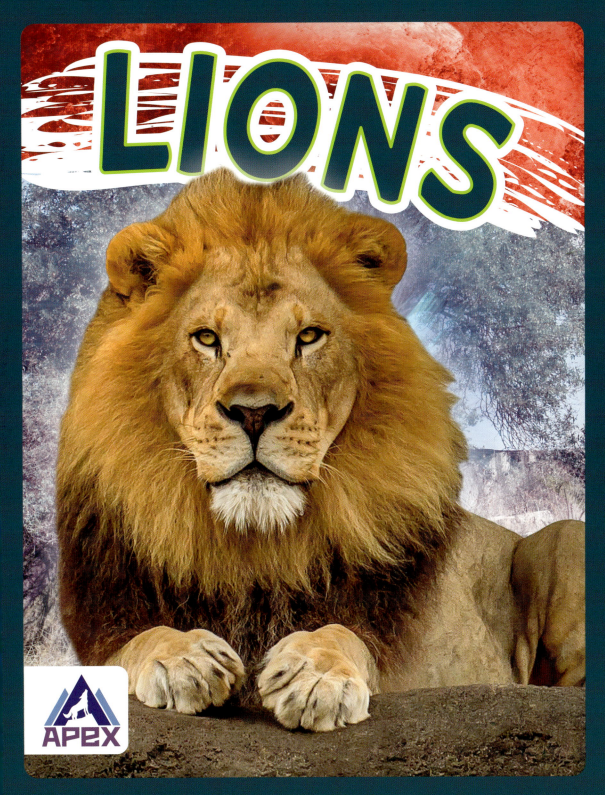

LIONS

BY Sophie Geister-Jones

WWW.APEXEDITIONS.COM

Copyright © 2022 by Apex Editions, Mendota Heights, MN 55120. All rights reserved. No part of this book may be reproduced or utilized in any form or by any means without written permission from the publisher.

Apex is distributed by North Star Editions:
sales@northstareditions.com | 888-417-0195

Produced for Apex by Red Line Editorial.

Photographs ©: Shutterstock Images, cover, 1, 12–13, 14–15, 16–17, 20–21, 22–23; iStockphoto, 4–5, 6–7, 8–9, 10–11, 14, 18, 19, 24, 24–25, 26–27, 29

Library of Congress Control Number: 2020952944

ISBN
978-1-63738-032-1 (hardcover)
978-1-63738-068-0 (paperback)
978-1-63738-136-6 (ebook pdf)
978-1-63738-104-5 (hosted ebook)

Printed in the United States of America
Mankato, MN
082021

NOTE TO PARENTS AND EDUCATORS

Apex books are designed to build literacy skills in striving readers. Exciting, high-interest content attracts and holds readers' attention. The text is carefully leveled to allow students to achieve success quickly. Additional features, such as bolded glossary words for difficult terms, help build comprehension.

TABLE OF CONTENTS

CHAPTER 1
KING OF THE BEASTS 5

CHAPTER 2
LIFE IN THE WILD 11

CHAPTER 3
STRONG BODIES 17

CHAPTER 4
HOW LIONS HUNT 23

Comprehension Questions • 28

Glossary • 30

To Learn More • 31

About the Author • 31

Index • 32

CHAPTER 1
KING OF THE BEASTS

A lion raises his head. A cool breeze blows through his mane. He sees another lion approach. He stands up.

Male lions start growing manes when they are about one year old.

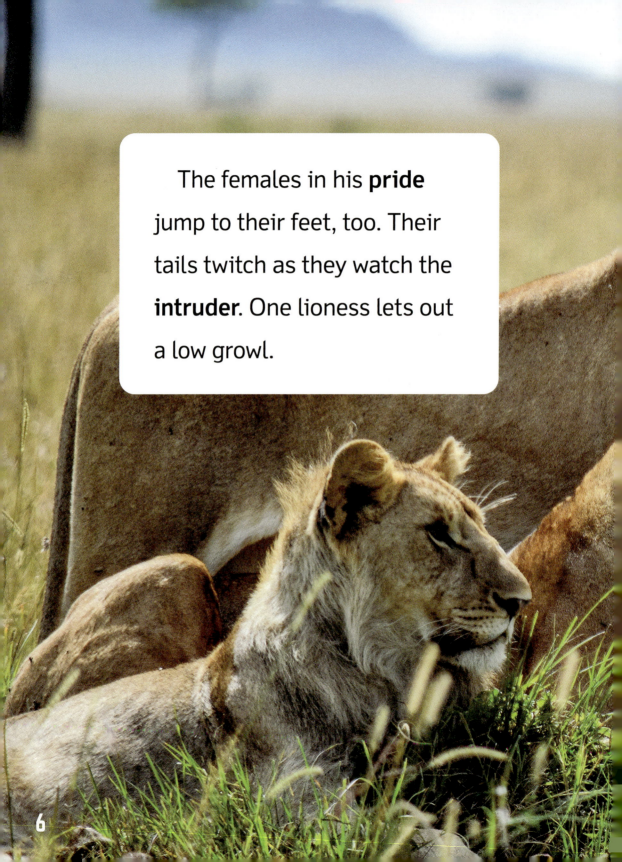

The females in his **pride** jump to their feet, too. Their tails twitch as they watch the **intruder**. One lioness lets out a low growl.

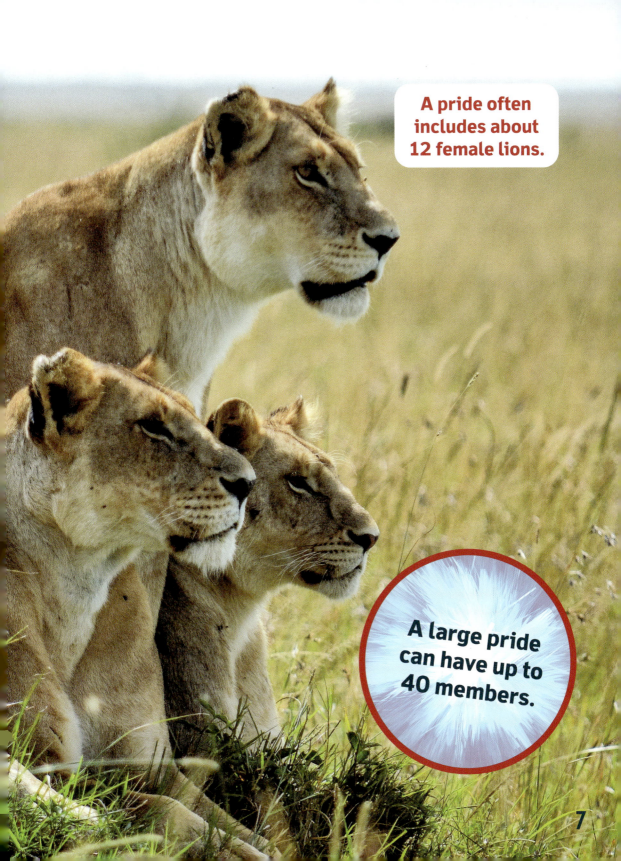

A pride often includes about 12 female lions.

A large pride can have up to 40 members.

Lions can tell how large another pride is by the sounds of its members' roars.

The lion opens his mouth and roars. Several lionesses join him. The sound fills the air. It is a warning. The intruder runs away.

LET IT ROAR

A lion's roar is loud. It can be heard from 5 miles (8 km) away. Lions roar to show their **territory**. They also roar at night before they hunt.

CHAPTER 2
LIFE IN THE WILD

Most lions live south of the Sahara Desert in Africa. They **roam** grasslands, **brush**, and **woodlands**.

A pride's territory can be up to 100 square miles (259 sq km).

Unlike most big cats, lions live in groups. These groups are called prides. Each pride is made mostly of females and their cubs.

Mother lions teach their cubs to hunt.

LIONS IN INDIA

One group of lions lives in India. These lions are smaller than lions in Africa. There are just a few hundred left in the wild. Male and female lions live separately. The females lead their own prides.

Female lions do most of the hunting. They raise the cubs, too. Male lions defend the pride. They make sure the cubs are safe.

Male lions guard their cubs from other males that want to take over the pride.

A pride often includes two or three male lions. They work together to guard the group.

Female lions leave their cubs to hunt.

CHAPTER 3
STRONG BODIES

Lions are top **predators**. They have big **muscles**. They have large heads. Their strong jaws help them catch and kill **prey**.

A lion's teeth can be almost 4 inches (10 cm) long.

A lion's coat can be shades of yellow or brown. These colors help the lion blend in with its surroundings.

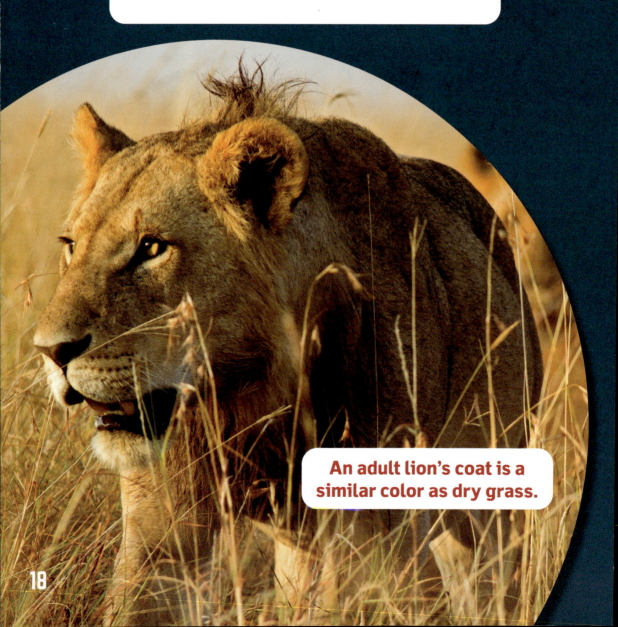

An adult lion's coat is a similar color as dry grass.

Lions sometimes climb trees. One reason is to avoid swarms of biting flies.

A lion cub's spots help it hide.

BABY LIONS

Lion cubs are born with black spots. The spots fade as the cubs get older. Most females stay with the pride when they grow up. Males leave after about two years.

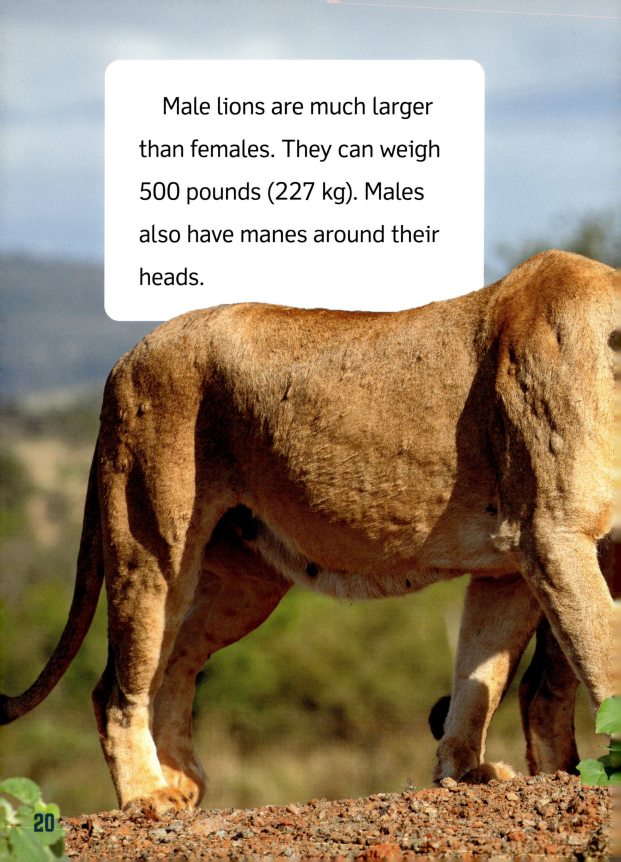

Male lions are much larger than females. They can weigh 500 pounds (227 kg). Males also have manes around their heads.

A male lion's mane helps it attract female lions.

Lions with darker manes tend to be stronger.

CHAPTER 4
HOW LIONS HUNT

Lions mainly eat antelopes, wildebeests, and zebras. Lions hide in places they know animals visit. They wait for animals to come. Then they charge.

Lions eat every three to four days.

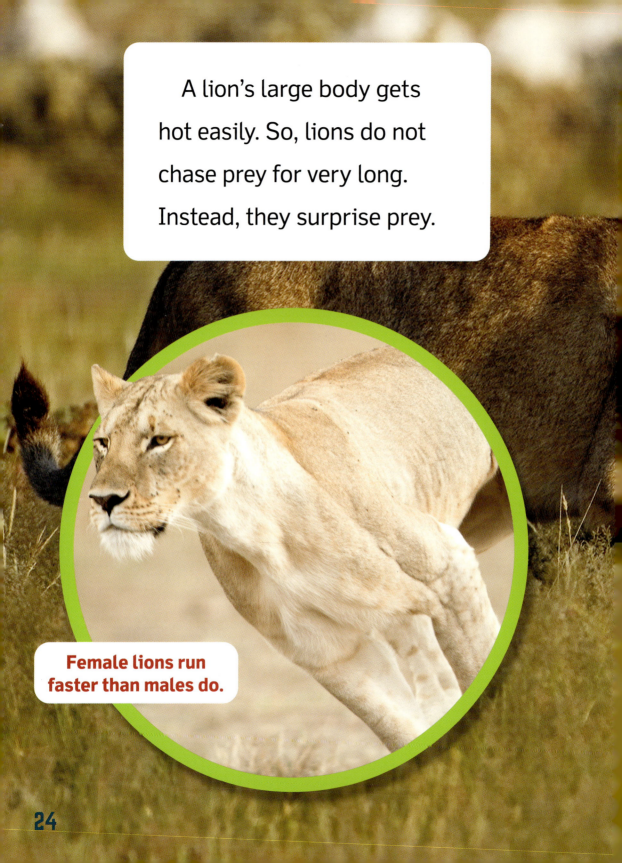

A lion's large body gets hot easily. So, lions do not chase prey for very long. Instead, they surprise prey.

Female lions run faster than males do.

Lions stay low and hidden as they sneak up on prey.

Lions sleep about 20 hours each day.

Lions swipe at an animal to knock it down. Then they bite its neck. Lions hunt in groups. They work together to take down big animals.

Lions use their sharp claws to grab prey.

BIG EATERS

Lions eat huge amounts of food in one sitting. Some lions can eat 95 pounds (43 kg) of meat in a day. Their stomachs stretch out to make room for all the food.

COMPREHENSION QUESTIONS

Write your answers on a separate piece of paper.

1. Write a sentence describing how lions hunt their prey.

2. Lions live and hunt in groups. Would you rather work alone or with a group? Why?

3. How many hours do lions sleep each day?
- **A.** 5 hours
- **B.** 12 hours
- **C.** 20 hours

4. Why do lions hunt in groups?
- **A.** Working together helps them catch bigger animals.
- **B.** Working together helps them run a long time.
- **C.** Lions spend lots of time chasing their food.

5. What does **defend** mean in this book?

*Male lions **defend** the pride. They make sure the cubs are safe.*

    A. to guard something
    B. to try to hurt something
    C. to stay away from something

6. What does **shades** mean in this book?

*A lion's coat can be **shades** of yellow or brown.*

    A. higher or lower types of sound
    B. lighter or darker versions of a color
    C. places without much light

Answer key on page 32.

GLOSSARY

brush
Land covered in bushes and other short plants.

intruder
Someone or something that goes where it's not welcome, wanted, or supposed to be.

muscles
Parts of the body that help with strength and movement.

predators
Animals that hunt and eat other animals.

prey
An animal that is hunted and eaten by another animal.

pride
A group of lions.

roam
To move throughout a large area.

swarms
Large groups of insects, especially insects that move and fly together.

territory
An area that an animal or group of animals lives in and defends.

woodlands
Areas with many trees.

TO LEARN MORE

BOOKS

Duling, Kaitlyn. *African Lions.* Minneapolis: Bellwether Media, 2020.

Meinking, Mary. *Lions.* Lake Elmo, MN: Focus Readers, 2018.

Sommer, Nathan. *Lion vs. Hyena Clan.* Minneapolis: Bellwether Media, 2020.

ONLINE RESOURCES

Visit **www.apexeditions.com** to find links and resources related to this title.

ABOUT THE AUTHOR

Sophie Geister-Jones lives in Saint Paul, Minnesota. She loves reading. She and her brothers have a book club.

INDEX

A
Africa, 11, 13

B
brush, 11

C
colors, 18
cubs, 12, 14, 19

E
eating, 23, 27

F
females, 6, 12–14, 19–20

G
grasslands, 11

H
hunting, 9, 14, 26

I
India, 13

J
jaws, 17

M
males, 13–15, 19–20
mane, 5, 20–21

P
prey, 17, 24
prides, 6–7, 12–15, 19

R
roar, 9

S
Sahara Desert, 11
spots, 19
stomachs, 27

T
territory, 9

Answer Key:
1. Answers will vary; **2.** Answers will vary; **3.** C; **4.** A; **5.** A; **6.** B